Wisconsin

WISCONSIN

1848

A Buddy Book
by

Julie Murray

ABDO
Publishing Company

VISIT US AT

www.abdopub.com

Published by ABDO Publishing Company, 4940 Viking Drive, Edina, Minnesota 55435.

Printed in the United States.

Edited by: Sarah Tieck
Contributing Editor: Michael P. Goecke
Graphic Design: Deb Coldiron, Maria Hosley
Image Research: Sarah Tieck
Photographs: AP/Wide World, BrandX, Clipart.com, Getty Images, Library of Congress, One Mile Up, Photodisc, Photos.com, Scenicphoto.com, Special Thanks to the National Scenic Byways Program (www.byways.com) for use of the photo on page 20, Wisconsin Dept. of Tourism

Library of Congress Cataloging-in-Publication Data

Murray, Julie, 1969-
   Wisconsin / Julie Murray.
      p. cm. — (The United States)
   Includes index.
   Contents: A snapshot of Wisconsin — Where is Wisconsin? — All about Wisconsin — Cities and the capital _ Famous citizens — Wisconsin's landscape — Farming in Wisconsin — Wisconsin Dells — A history of Wisconsin.
   ISBN 1-59197-708-8
      1. Wisconsin—Juvenile literature. I. Title.

F581.3.M87 2005
977.5—dc22

                                                    2005048086

Table Of Contents

A Snapshot Of Wisconsin

When people think of Wisconsin, they think of cheese and milk. This is because Wisconsin is known as the dairy capital of America. The state is a leading producer of the nation's cheese.

Farms are important to the state of Wisconsin.

4

Wisconsin's nickname is "The Badger State." A badger is a small animal that lives in holes and tunnels in the ground. The nickname refers to lead miners from the 1800s. The miners dug into Wisconsin's hillsides looking for lead. This reminded people of how badgers dig into the ground.

Wisconsin became the 30th state on May 29, 1848. Wisconsin has 56,145 square miles (145,415 sq km) of land. It is the 26th-largest state. Wisconsin is home to 5,363,675 people.

Where Is Wisconsin?

There are four parts of the United States. Each part is called a region. Each region is in a different area of the country. The United States Census Bureau says the four regions are the Northeast, the South, the Midwest, and the West.

Wisconsin is located in the Midwest region of the United States. The seasons are spring, summer, fall, and winter. Sometimes, Wisconsin has severe weather. This includes floods in the spring, tornadoes in the summer, and blizzards in the winter.

It often snows during the winter months in Wisconsin.

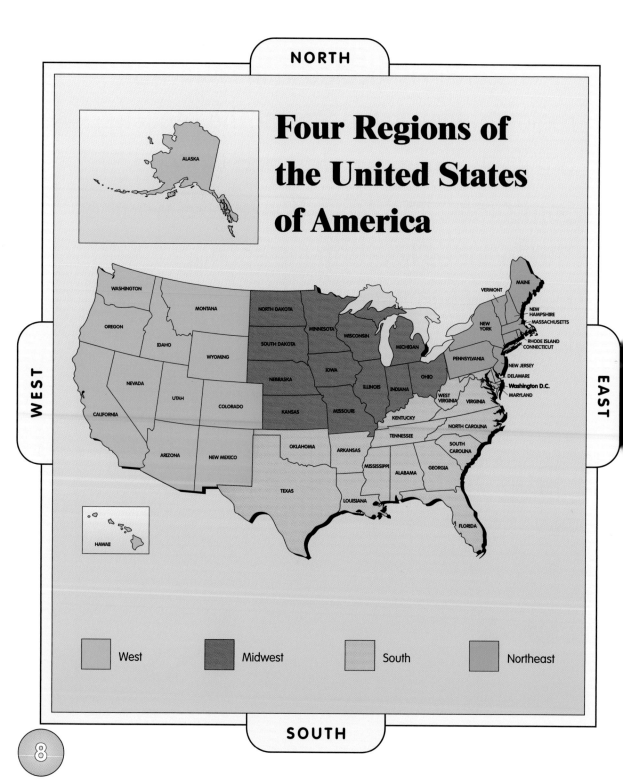

Four Regions of the United States of America

ALASKA

WASHINGTON
MONTANA
NORTH DAKOTA
MINNESOTA
VERMONT
MAINE

OREGON
IDAHO
WYOMING
SOUTH DAKOTA
WISCONSIN
MICHIGAN
NEW YORK
NEW HAMPSHIRE
MASSACHUSETTS

NEVADA
UTAH
COLORADO
NEBRASKA
IOWA
ILLINOIS
INDIANA
OHIO
PENNSYLVANIA
RHODE ISLAND
CONNECTICUT
NEW JERSEY
DELAWARE
Washington D.C.
MARYLAND

CALIFORNIA
KANSAS
MISSOURI
WEST VIRGINIA
VIRGINIA

ARIZONA
NEW MEXICO
OKLAHOMA
ARKANSAS
KENTUCKY
TENNESSEE
NORTH CAROLINA
SOUTH CAROLINA

TEXAS
LOUISIANA
MISSISSIPPI
ALABAMA
GEORGIA

FLORIDA

HAWAII

West   Midwest   South   Northeast

Wisconsin is bordered by four other states and two of the five Great Lakes. Minnesota and Iowa are west. Illinois is south. Michigan is northeast. Lake Superior is north. Lake Michigan is east.

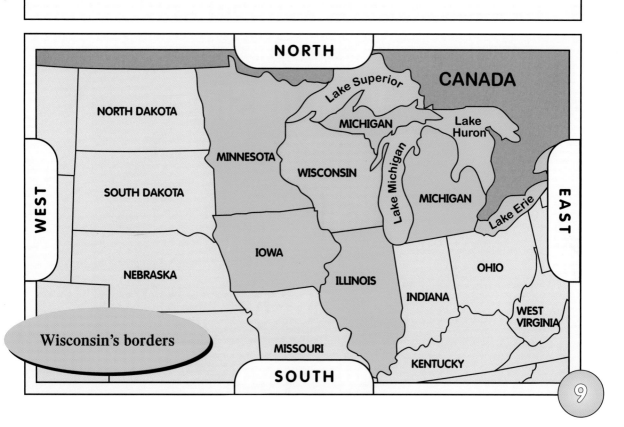

Wisconsin's borders

Wisconsin

State abbreviation: WI

State nickname: The Badger State

State capital: Madison

State motto: Forward

Statehood: May 29, 1848, 30th state

Population: 5,363,675, ranks 18th

State flag:
Adopted in 1913

WISCONSIN

FORWARD

1848

Land area: 56,145 square miles (145,415 sq km), ranks 26th

State tree: Sugar maple

State song: "On, Wisconsin!"

State government: Three branches: legislative, executive, and judicial

Average July temperature: 70°F (21°C)

Average January temperature: 14°F (-10°C)

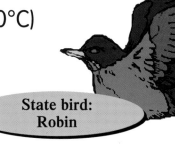
State bird: Robin

State animal: Badger

State flower: Wood violet

Cities And The Capital

Madison is the capital city of Wisconsin. It is the second-largest city in the state. Madison is located in the south-central part of Wisconsin. The city is located between three lakes. These are Lake Mendota, Lake Monona, and Lake Wingra. The University of Wisconsin-Madison campus is in Madison.

Wisconsin's State Capitol

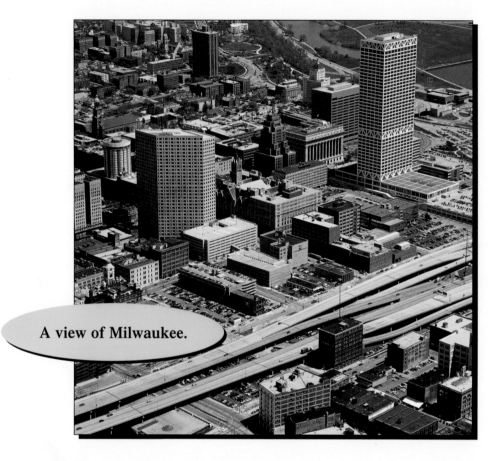

A view of Milwaukee.

Milwaukee is the largest city in the state. This city is located on the shores of Lake Michigan. This is one of the five Great Lakes. The Milwaukee River also flows through this city.

Famous Citizens

Frank Lloyd Wright (1867–1959)

Frank Lloyd Wright was born in Richland Center. He built his famous house, Taliesin, in Spring Green. Wright was a famous architect. He is known for designing buildings that blended in with the landscape. This is known as prairie style. Wright designed many buildings all over the world. Some famous buildings include the Guggenheim Museum in New York City, and the Marin County Civic Center in California.

Frank Lloyd Wright

Famous Citizens

Vince Lombardi (1913–1970)

Vince Lombardi was born in New York City in 1913. But he is very famous in Wisconsin. Lombardi lived in Green Bay. He was the coach of the Green Bay Packers from 1959 to 1968. After retiring, he worked as general manager. The team won the first two Super Bowls during this time. These were in 1967 and 1968.

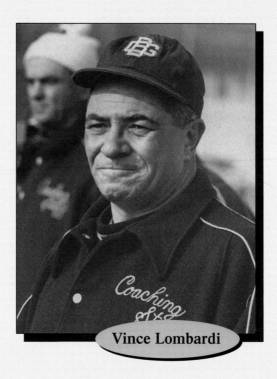

Vince Lombardi

Wisconsin's Landscape

The state of Wisconsin is shaped like a mitten. The thumb of the mitten juts out into Lake Michigan. This is called the Door Peninsula. This area has rugged coastline and thick forests. It is a popular tourist destination.

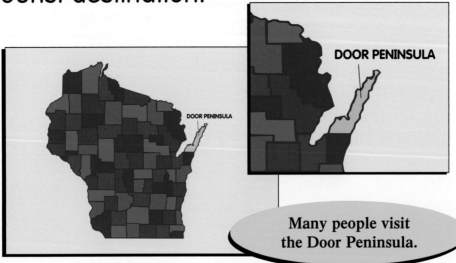

DOOR PENINSULA

DOOR PENINSULA

Many people visit the Door Peninsula.

Many different crops are grown on Wisconsin's farmland.

Southeastern Wisconsin has some of the state's best farmland. Lake Winnebago is found in east-central Wisconsin. It is the largest natural lake in the state.

The northern part of Wisconsin borders Lake Superior. Lake Superior is one of the five Great Lakes. It is also the largest freshwater lake in the world. The Apostle Islands are there. This area is another popular tourist destination.

A view of the Apostle Islands
and Lake Superior.

A view of the
Mississippi River in Wisconsin.

Timms Hill is the highest point in the state. It stands 1,952 feet (595 m) tall. It is found in Chequamegon-Nicolet National Forest in north-central Wisconsin.

The southwestern part of Wisconsin has rugged cliffs with deep valleys. The Mississippi River runs along the state's border in this area.

Farming In Wisconsin

Wisconsin is called America's Dairyland. More than 35 percent of the farms in Wisconsin raise dairy cows. Today, Wisconsin is a leading producer of cheese in America. It is also one of the leading producers of other dairy foods, such as milk and butter.

The state of Wisconsin
is known for its dairy farms.

Corn grows in fields like this one.

Almost half of the land in Wisconsin is used for farming. Farmers grow fruits, vegetables, and field crops. The leading crop in Wisconsin is corn. Wisconsin farmers also grow soybeans, cranberries, hay, wheat, and apples.

Wisconsin Dells

The Wisconsin River runs through the center of Wisconsin. Part of the river flows through a deep, narrow canyon. This is called the Wisconsin Dells. It is known for its scenery. The views come from unusual rock formations and sandstone cliffs.

A view of the Wisconsin Dells.

People view the rock formations in the Wisconsin Dells from special boats.

Today, the Wisconsin Dells is a popular vacation spot. Families go there to see the scenery. Also, there are several water parks, boat rides, live shows, and amusement parks with roller coasters and go-karts.

Wisconsin

1634: French explorer Jean Nicolet arrives in Wisconsin.

1673: Jacques Marquette and Louis Jolliet explore Wisconsin's rivers.

1848: Wisconsin becomes the 30th state on May 29.

1854: A meeting in Wisconsin leads to the start of the Republican Party.

1871: The Peshtigo forest fire kills more than 1,000 people. The fire also destroys several towns in northeastern Wisconsin.

1967: The Green Bay Packers win the first Super Bowl.

1998: Wisconsin celebrates its 150th anniversary of being a state.

Tommy Thompson

2001: Wisconsin governor Tommy Thompson becomes the United States Secretary of Health and Human Services.

2005: Milwaukee hosts the 154th Wisconsin State Fair.

Cities In Wisconsin

Superior

Peshtigo

Eau Claire

Green Bay

Richland Center

Spring Green

Sun Prairie

Madison

Milwaukee

Important Words

blizzard a heavy snowstorm with strong winds.

capital a city where government leaders meet.

nickname a name that describes something special about a person or a place.

peninsula a piece of land surrounded by water on three sides.

tornado a storm cloud that is shaped like a funnel and swirls fast, destroying homes and cities.

Web Sites

To learn more about Wisconsin, visit ABDO Publishing Company on the World Wide Web. Web site links about Wisconsin are featured on our Book Links page. These links are routinely monitored and updated to provide the most current information available.

www.abdopub.com

Index